THE PEOPLE OF THE WAY

Martin Nyanzu

WestBow Press books may be ordered through booksellers or by contacting:

WestBow Press
A Division of Thomas Nelson & Zondervan
1663 Liberty Drive
Bloomington, IN 47403
www.westbowpress.com
844-714-3454

Scripture quotations marked (NIV) are taken from the Holy Bible, NEW INTERNATIONAL VERSION®, NIV® Copyright © 1973, 1978, 1984, 2011 by Biblica, Inc.® Used by permission. All rights reserved worldwide.

Scriptures marked (NLT) are taken from the Holy Bible, New Living Translation, copyright © 1996, 2004, 2015 by Tyndale House Foundation. Used by permission of Tyndale House Publishers Inc., Carol Stream, Illinois 60188. All rights reserved.

Scriptures quoted from the International Children's Bible®, copyright ©1986, 1988, 1999, 2015 by Tommy Nelson. Used by permission.

ISBN: 978-1-6642-9702-9 (sc)
ISBN: 978-1-6642-9703-6 (e)

Library of Congress Control Number: 2023906406

Print information available on the last page.

WestBow Press rev. date: 06/22/2023

WESTBOW
P R E S S®
A DIVISION OF THOMAS NELSON
& ZONDERVAN

To our children who are growing up in a culture that is constantly resisting the way – Josette, Jeffrey, Matthias & Malachi.

THE WAY

"Jesus answered, "I am the way and the truth and the life. No one comes to the Father except through me" (John 14:6 NIV)

Once upon a time, Jesus knew when he was going to die and decided to tell his friends who were also his followers, they called him master. During their talk, Jesus told them they know the way to the place he would be going after his death. Thomas was not sure about this and asked Jesus saying 'Lord, we don't know where you would be going, so how can we know the way? Thomas always had questions. He always wanted to understand what was going on.

After Jesus died, the Holy Spirit from God miraculously brought him out of the grave in a new body. He showed himself to his friends and followers for 40 days. He shared many secrets of his Kingdom with them. One of the secrets he shared was the coming of the Holy Spirit. Jesus told them to wait for him in a special place so that they could receive the promised Holy Spirit. Guess what! They obeyed and waited. When the Holy Spirit came upon them, he gave them ability to go everywhere to tell people about Jesus. Everywhere they went, people called them "the people of the way" This is because, they acted, talked and did things like Jesus. Today, another word for "people of the way" is Christians. People who act, talk and do things like Jesus are called Christians because they are "Christ-like". Therefore, a Christian is a person who acts, talks and does everything according to the teachings of Jesus.

After the death of Jesus, and the coming of the Holy Spirit, the friends and followers of Jesus saw many good changes in their lives. They started doing things they could not do before. They became bold, willing to share all that they saw Jesus do and teach, even when they were told not to. Even though they saw Jesus do many miracles, sometimes, they were not sure who He really was. But to them, the greatest of all the miracles Jesus did was telling them he would die and rise on the third day and actually doing it.

THE ONLY WAY

"Jesus is the only One who can save people. No one else in the world is able to save us." (Acts 4:12 ICB)

The friends of Jesus who went about telling everyone about Jesus were called apostles, meaning someone who is sent to finish a task. However, there were other men and women who helped the apostles to finish the task of telling everyone about Jesus, they were called disciples, another word for followers. The apostles who were sure they saw Jesus rise from the dead went about telling everyone that Jesus is the only way to heaven because he died and rose again. This is why after we die in this body, we shall still have life and live again forever. But this is only possible if we believe that Jesus is our master and that he died for us. I will tell you more about what it means for Jesus to die for us later on, and what his death has done for us.

Since the days of the apostles till today, anyone who has become a follower of Jesus keeps sharing with people that Jesus is the only way, but sometimes people are not happy about this statement. This is because there were other human masters who lived and had followers. Some of them are Muhammed who founded Islam, Buddha who founded Buddhism and Krishna who founded Hinduism. They taught their followers somethings too but if we compare them to Jesus we run into a problem. This is why Christians always share that Jesus is the only way. Even though, today, some people do not like Jesus, they still believe that he has helped us a lot more than Muhammed, Buddha and Krishna all put together.

Before we compare Jesus, Muhammed, Buddha and Krishna, let us look at something every human being believes in this world. This will help us to know why one of these leaders is the only one who can save us. Everyone in the world believes that they are not perfect because they have been wrong in the past, or continue to do something wrong every day. Let us think for a bit, If someone does something wrong and stands before a judge, what do you think will happen? If the judge is a good judge, he or she will have to do something about it. The wrong we have all done and continue to do is called sin. Sin does not allow us to be good friends with God because He hates sin. Staying away from God because of sin leads to death. Everyone wants to do what is right and good, but we are not able to do this for a long time before we do the wrong thing again. Because of this problem, we needed someone to come and die for us so that instead of us dying forever, he would give his life for us and die in our place. This is a gift Muhammed, Buddha and Krishna could not give any human being. Only Jesus has done this for all of us, even those who do not believe in him yet.

Remember I promised I will tell you more about what the death of Jesus has done for us? Well, this is the time. Muhammed, Buddha and Krishna are dead but could not rise from the dead. If they did, they would have had power over death. That would mean that their followers would have lived by believing in them even if they died in this body. Don't forget when we die in this body, we will live again. Because of what we know now, that was why when Jesus died and rose again, the people at the time who did not believe in him tried all they could to say that he did not rise. They tried to give some people free money to say that Jesus did not rise. They also killed many people to make the followers of Jesus afraid, but the more they did this the more a lot of people came to accept that Jesus died and rose again. When Muhammed, Buddha and Krishna died, nobody tried to give anybody free money or kill people to stop others from knowing about them. The death and rising of Jesus mean our sins are forgiving. It also means we will live even if we die in this body, this gives us hope. This is why a true Christian is full of hope even when they are about to die or on their death bed.

THE MESSAGE OF THE WAY

"Therefore, go and make disciples of all the nations, baptizing them in the name of the Father and the Son and the Holy Spirit. Teach these new disciples to obey all the commands I have given you. And be sure of this: I am with you always, even to the end of the age." (Matt 28:19-20 NLT)

After Jesus was born and grew, he said and did things that no man has been able to do. For example, he said things like "I came to seek and save the lost" (Luke 19:10 NIV), "if you have seen me, you have seen the Father" (John 14:9 CEV), "your sins are forgiven" (Luke 7:48 NIV), "receive your sight" (Luke 18:42 NIV), and many more. He also raised people from the dead, gave food to 5000 people from 5 loaves of bread and 2 fish. Jesus did and said so many things that all of them would not fit in the Bible. Because of these things, many people became free, hopeful and could do the things God wanted them to do. Buddha, Muhammed and Krishna put together could not do anything close to what Jesus did.

When the apostles and disciples went about telling people about Jesus, they first of all asked people everywhere to repent from their sins. After that, they told them to believe in Jesus alone, and nobody else, why? Because it was Jesus who said he would die and rise again, and he did, and gave life to everyone. The apostles were surprised to see that whenever they told people to believe in Jesus, the same miracles Jesus did and even more happened. The eyes of the blind opened, the sick got healed, the dead were raised, sins were forgiven, and people's lives changed for good.

EVERYONE IS GOING SOMEWHERE

"Everyone must die once. After a person dies, he is judged" (Hebrews 9:27 ICB)

If you have looked carefully, you would notice that sometimes people are born into the world and sometimes people die. Where did people come from? Why are they born into this world, why do they have to be nice to each other, and where are they going after they die? These are questions only Jesus and his followers can answer very well, why? This is because of where Jesus came from, what he came to do in this world, how he treated people, and where he is now after he died and rose again.

Jesus came from God, who created all people just like him. Therefore, we all come from God. We came into this world to do what would bring honor to God just as Jesus did. Because we all came from God, then we are to treat people in a good way by knowing what is right and wrong. Our knowledge of what is right and wrong depends on God because we are made just like him. Because Jesus died and rose again, we will also rise again and spend the rest of our days with Jesus. So where is everyone going after they die? If you answered to be with Jesus, you are right, but I am sad to say that some are not on the right way.

If your parents ask you to follow them and you agree to follow them everywhere they go, that will mean that if they step out of the house, you would also step out of the house. If they go to the mall, you would go to the mall with them, if they go to the library, you would go to the library with them. It is the same way with Jesus, Muhammed, Krishna and Buddha. What they taught their followers will tell where their followers would be after they die. If I had time to tell you all about the teachings of Jesus, Krishna, Muhammed and Buddha, you would know that all of them did not teach the same things. Sometimes, people have made a mistake to think that they all taught us the same things. This is why some people don't like it when someone says, "Jesus is the only way". Jesus, Muhammed, Krishna, and Buddha cannot lead us to the same place, especially when their teachings are not the same. Something is either right or wrong, left or right, day or night, dead or alive. A person cannot be going in the right and wrong direction at the same time or left and right at the same time or be dead and alive at the same time.

CHALLENGES ALONG THE WAY

"Jesus answered: "Be careful that no one fools you. Many people will come in my name. They will say, 'I am the Christ.' And they will fool many people"
(Matt 24:4-5 ICB)

One of the teachings of Jesus, which the people of the way believed and shared with others is that when someone decides to follow Jesus, a lot of things in this world will try so hard to get them not to follow Jesus who is the only way. When you sit in your car with your parents to go to school or church, you will drive by houses, other cars, traffic lights, trees and sometimes you will drive through a pothole on the road. It is the same with Christians who are travelling through this world to be with Jesus after they die. Because Jesus is the only way that gives us life, we want to do our very best not to get off the right way.

Today, a lot of people who are not on the right way to Jesus are on another way that will not give them life after they die. Sometimes, they get on the wrong way through what they see and learn from T.V, TikTok, Facebook, Instagram, Tweeter, YouTube and other social media platforms. There are some good things on these platforms, however, everyone will agree that majority of the things there do not match the teachings of Jesus. The pictures, videos and things people share on social media shows that if we compare the teachings of Jesus, Muhammed, Buddha and Krishna, only Jesus' teaching is able to truly tell us the state of the human heart. Because Jesus is God and created us, he is the only one who knows what is in our heart. Jesus said the human heart is evil and can lie. That means sometimes, when you think you are ok, you are actually not ok. Sometimes, you can say to yourself, you will not do something again and then you find yourself doing it, or sometimes, you say you have forgiven someone only to know that you only said it but you have not forgiven. Because Jesus got these things right in addition to many other things, Christians conclude that he is different. When someone tells you everything about you as it is and also has the power over death and life, the right thing you will do is to give your life to him. Giving your life to Jesus means you have decided to believe that all that you have heard about Jesus is the truth, that he died for you, that he was buried, that he rose on the third day, that if you believe in him your sins will be forgiven.

WHY SOME ARE NOT ON THE RIGHT WAY

"Some people think they are doing what's right. But what they are doing will really kill them" (Proverbs 14:12 ICB)

You will be surprised to know that there are about 8 billion people in the world today according to those who count people. More people worship Jesus than Muhammed, Buddha and Krishna, but you should not be happy about this because if you divide 8 billion into four, three out of four don't' know Jesus. This means many people are not on the right way. There are a few reasons why many people are not on the right way.

- Some were born into homes that are not Christian
- Some have not heard anyone talk to them about Jesus
- Some have heard about Jesus but because of the teachings of Muhammed, Buddha and Krishna they have not decided yet, though a lot more people have left Muhammed, Buddha and Krishna and become followers of Jesus
- Some have not become Christians because of the behavior of some who say they follow Jesus but do not live like Jesus
- Some have not become followers of Jesus because of their heart. Their heart is misleading them that Jesus is not the way. They think they can find their own way without Jesus. Because Jesus is always right, these people need help.

PREPARING THE WAY

"There is a voice of a man who calls out in the desert: 'Prepare the way for the Lord. Make the road straight for him" (Mark 1:3 ICB)

The People of the Way are not sure what age a child has to be to accept the teachings of Jesus. However, the Bible teaches that when a child is old enough to know right from wrong and can understand what they have heard about Jesus, then the time is right. Are you sure you can share what you have learned about Jesus from this book with your parents? then you must first pray to Jesus and ask him to come and live in your heart and change you like he did to the apostles and the disciples. After that, start talking to your parents about your next step. You could be the next child Jesus would use to bring the rest of the billions who have not heard about Jesus yet into his Kingdom. God always works through young people for the following reasons

- It is easy for them to trust
- They have not been through a lot of problems in life
- They believe very easily and strongly
- Most young people know they came from God

Until you are guided by an adult the right way to accept Jesus, keep on praying about what you have come to know from this book about Jesus, watch only movies that will help you know more about Jesus, listen to only songs that talks about Jesus, your use of social media should not take you away from the right way when the time comes for your parents to allow you to go there. Whenever you are on social media, know that you are a follower of Jesus Christ, you must do what the early followers of Jesus did.

If you ever get the chance to share Jesus with anyone, do not force them to accept Jesus because truth must never be forced. When the right time comes, share what you know about Jesus to anyone who asks for the hope that you have in him. Jesus said nobody can come to him unless he calls the person in his heart. Whenever you share anything about Jesus to someone, you must give room to Jesus to do his work after you have done yours. Don't forget to pray for people before and after you have spoken to them about Jesus. You must know that there is a right time and a right place to talk about Jesus. For example, when you are doing something, you must finish in a certain time, think about finishing it. There is time for everything. A couple of the very good times to talk to people about Jesus will be when they ask you anything about Jesus, or when someone is sick. This could be a family member of someone you know who is not a follower of Jesus. Anytime you get the chance to share about Jesus, you are preparing the way for Jesus to enter into the person's heart.

CONCLUSION

All people everywhere have sinned. If you were to ask the person next to you, they will tell you they have done something wrong in the past. This is why Jesus came to die for us. We needed someone to save us from our sins. Jesus is the only one who has been able to die for us and rose on the third day. His death has paid for our sins. Before he came, a lot of prophets gave us promises about how he would be born. They even told us about where he would be born, the things he would do, how he would die and how he would rise again. When he came, he did and taught exactly the way the prophets said. This made people wonder if he was the one the prophets spoke about. People started believing him because they saw him heal the sick, set people free, raise the dead and teach people in a way nobody ever did. Some of his followers saw all these things yet were still not fully sure about who he was until he died and rose again. After Jesus died and rose again, nobody could change the minds of his followers and friends about who he was.

Jesus' followers were ready to talk to everyone they met about who Jesus was. They were even ready to die because of him. After talking to people about Jesus, they saw people getting healed, blind eyes opening, and many people coming to Jesus just as Jesus told them. Throughout human history, there has not been any single person who has changed the world the way Jesus has done. Some have not accepted him yet because of where they were born, what other Christians have done to them, or they are just not ready because their heart is misleading them, or nobody has shared Jesus with them yet. Jesus can use young people to prepare the heart of those he wants to call unto himself. Are you ready to be on the way and help get others on the way as well?

nted in the United States
Baker & Taylor Publisher Services